BRAIN ON FIRE

Unleashing Your Creative Superpowers

JoAnn R. Corley

Brain on Fire – Unleashing Your Creative Superpowers

Written by: JoAnn R. Corley

To order this book visit www.thehumansphere.com
All rights reserved.
SBN-13: 978-1512288773
ISBN-10: 1512288772

"Human creativity is virtually a limitless resource."
-Rise of the Creative Class, Richard Florida

Contents_____

Act III - Your Creativity Toolkit
To build the flame and stoke its power, it's worth it to collect a variety of woods. 71

Epilogue - Curtain Call
It's worth it to keep the embers glowing. 99

About the Author 105

Dedicated to all who wish to be fully alive!

"Let's go invent tomorrow rather than worrying about what happened yesterday."

- Steve Jobs

| Preface

I remember many camping trips as a young teenager. It grew to be a love that carried into my adult life.

Besides the sheer joy I developed being in nature, detached from the everyday bustle and grind, I loved the challenge of living off the land – sort of. I wasn't hard core but a practiced novice at the basics; gathering firewood, cooking everything over an open fire, including coffee with an old camping coffee pot. I loved setting up the tent, preparing the sleeping bags and arranging the campsite to get the best cozy, campy feeling possible.

My particular pleasure was the challenge of starting a fire without cheating. Cheating involved newspaper or lighter fluid. That would feel like utter defeat and an insult to fellow tent campers everywhere. No, it had to be started with authentic elements of the woods.

I began with the thinnest, tiniest twigs assembled in a square, "teepee" type formation with such delicate precision, one match (yes the one modern allowance) was all you needed to ignite what grew into a large, blazing fire.

The key to the success of what I eventually termed "the one match challenge" was the choices of twigs, their strategic arrangement and the deliberate timing and addition of certain sized twigs. One twig too big or a formation that didn't allow enough oxygen and the match flame would quickly peter out.

I see a significant similarity with another love of mine, helping people discover and connect with their creative power. I see the act of generating ideas, engaging in the creative experience much the same as starting a campfire. It takes the right conditions with the right elements combined with a strategic method (and a few other components) to get a blazing, sustaining, fire of ideas going.

I've discovered most people don't know that. People in general and leaders of companies need to know that now more than ever.

Or, they may have experienced small, periodic flames that can be easily doused, but they really don't know how to build or have rarely encountered a substantial, sustaining fire. Many have no idea what's possible. Because of that, company leaders have no idea the amount of money left on the table – the profits never realized.

Many don't know how to build the type of fire that is raging, like one acting as nature's furnace on a cold, crisp night. They've not experienced one built so expertly that even in the morning glowing embers can be coaxed back to a breakfast fire with a few gentle puffs.

You know those kinds of fires – the stubborn ones. They're difficult to extinguish. They still have a few tiny tenacious flames persistently pushing through the wet ash determined to survive.

Most people have not encountered *that* kind of creative experience; like a substantial sustained campfire, sometimes raging when needed, yet embers continuously aglow.

It's the kind of experience *where...*
>   *there* is a constant source and steady flame of ideas

generating ideas feels so fun and effortless
the creative period wakes you up and keeps you up
what you produce surprises you, over and over again
you're in disbelief of what you're capable of
there is a creative flow so intense it's as if you're having
an out of body experience
you're so in the zone, you don't want to stop
you're in so deep, you loose track of time
the creative energy is so powerful, it's difficult to
extinguish

Everyone can and should have a creative experience like that!

This is your brain – on fire. It's my definition. I use it to remind
myself and articulate to others the scope and intensity of what's
possible. This phrase dramatically represents the power of our
capability. **At full strength, it feels like a superpower**. Your
mind is so supercharged that whatever it's holding can't be
contained like a volcano ready to erupt.

| My Spark is Your Spark

Of course a fire can begin with a simple spark and I'm always
amazed at how quickly a spark can spread into a raging fire. A
spark with the right conditions can be unstoppable.

That's what I wish for this book. I've desired to write it for
sometime as a companion to my workshops and more generally
to provide a more accessible platform from which to proclaim its
essential messages.

This is not meant to be an exhaustive resource on creativity, but
a spark that with use can generate and sustain a continuous,

meaningful fire to serve exactly what you, your company or group needs. It's intent is to light your fire, so that you can light others.

It's designed is to be a non-academic (there are enough of those), simple, approachable, practical creativity manifesto -- a loyal talent companion.

Enjoy it alone or share and use it within a group. It's written for individuals, corporate leaders, teams and teens in a way that anyone can read and gain immediate benefit.

I want to help and inspire everyone to create and write a new story of their creative capability, the impact it can have and the contributions that can be made.

Consider it your handbook and workbook – your fire guide to igniting the flames of your talent – emboldening your sense of personal power.

"At first people refuse to believe that a strange new thing can be done. Then they see it can be done. Then it is done and the world wonders why it was not done centuries ago."

Frances Burnett
Author of The Secret Garden

Act I
The Creative Advantage –
Making the Case
Why bother collecting the tinder?

| Introduction

Creativity. Think of the word itself for a second. What does it mean to you? Who comes to mind as a creative leader, past or present? What are some companies that thrive on creative thinking? You see it at Apple, Google, and top advertising and marketing firms. Creative thinking is welcomed at places like these. But in many corporate cultures, creativity is *still* undervalued and greatly misunderstood!

Corporate America has historically shunned creative thinking under the old leadership model of command and control, especially from anyone lower than the very top of the totem pole. Those were the days of, "I think, I tell you, you do."

It's a shame really. For years many missed out because we're all creative and have an incredible ability to harness that creativity to positively influence our careers, relationships and overall life happiness.

"Creativity not tapped is talent and profits left on the table."

It's time for a change. It's time that everyone be creative and recognize their creativity. It's time for **you** to be creative! Whether you are looking for a raise, the ability to work for yourself from your own home, or looking to improve your quality of life, happiness, or whatever goals you may have, a little bit of creativity is often the very first step – though it may not be recognized as such.

Rethinking Creativity

For the moment, let's put aside any preconceived notions of what it means to be creative. It's not an ability reserved for artists, graphic designers, marketers, advertisers or CEOs (though CEOs are *screaming* for their organizations to become more creative. Yes they shun it and scream for it at the same time. We'll get to this a bit later).

Creativity is a powerful capability to nurture, develop and master no matter where you work, live or play. And a little bit of creativity can even change your life – just ask Bill Bowerman who co-found one of today's largest multinational corporations in part thanks to an idea he stumbled upon while eating a waffle. Sounds crazy right?

But where do you start? How do you become creative? Is it a learned skill? Join me as we explore creativity, where it comes from and why we all seem to lose it, and learn how to get it back to see things from completely new perspectives. This is the journey those who attend my workshops experience. The purpose of this book is to replicate the content as best we can (though nothing can replace the experience of the live workshop) and to use this as a supplement for those who've attended and need a refresher.

Debunking Creativity

Some reading this might be thinking, "Well not everyone is creative." Oh contraire my friend.

I begin my workshops with two initial, critical questions:
How many of you honestly believe you're creative?
Some attendees raise their hand.

And the follow up question, *"How many of you were kids?"*
Of course everyone raises his or her hand with some good laughs as well.

I continue…
"News flash, this is worth the price of admission to learn this today. The question is not whether you are or are not creative, but what have you done with your creativity since you've been a kid? The fact is every person here is creative. If you've been a kid, you **are** creative!"

This is *the* exciting and critical point -- everyone is creative in some way! It's consistently proven in my workshops. (In my workshops we don't "talk" about creativity, we experience it!)

The sad reality is not very people know it or believe it and even fewer have been taught how to exercise it – practically. This presents a significant challenge in our corporate environments and more broadly in our economy today.

> *"…an idea is an economic good –*
> *they create enormous wealth and value."*
> *-John Howskins, The Creative Economy*

Creative Thinking is a
Business & Economic Imperative

"Ideas are the new commodity of the 21st century."
-Richard Florida, Rise of The Creative Class

If companies and our U.S. economy are going to stay competitive, continue to grow at more than a snails pace (at least at the time of this writing) create jobs, cultivate our vast resources of human capital we've got to come to grips with our **creative deficit.** I believe we're experiencing a creativity crisis!

The creativity workshops I've conducted through-out North America over the past 15 plus years have provided substantial and practical evidence of the view of creativity among the typical worker. Thousands of employees from every sector of the economy from government to high tech have attended. With only a very few exceptions, the average number of those who honestly believed they're creative was about 1/4 to 1/3.

In fact just recently, I was conducting a creativity workshop for a company whose industry is going through some major changes. There were over 45 of their top leaders there and when asked, "How many of you honestly believe you are creative?" ...5 of the 45 raised their hand. Houston – we have a problem.

Why does that matter? If employees don't think or believe they are creative, there will be no attempt to be so.

And if a company's key leadership doesn't believe they are so, how can they lead effectively when responding to new, changing and challenging market demands?

Creativity is not reserved for the "artsy fartsy" folks! This belief truly blocks the non-artsy from embracing and tapping into their own creative potential. Essentially, **it is a critically relevant skill that must be incorporated into all company cultures** – from top leadership on down. It should no longer be seen as an unapproachable, optional capability, but a 21st century competency. In fact, there are some companies that have adopted this believe and include it in performance reviews.

Additionally, many leaders in our country have recognized how essential it is. In a study conducted by the IBM Leadership institute, it was revealed that 1500 CEO's identified creativity as *the most* essential leadership competency impacting the success of their companies going forward. I think that might surprise some.

"There is compelling new evidence that CEOs' priorities in this area are changing in important ways. According to a new survey of 1,500 chief executives conducted by IBM's Institute for Business Value (NYSE: IBM -News), CEOs identify "creativity" as the most important leadership competency for the successful enterprise of the future.

That's creativity—not operational effectiveness, influence, or even dedication. Coming out of the worst economic downturn in their professional lifetimes, when managerial discipline and rigor ruled the day, this indicates a remarkable shift in attitude. It is consistent with the study's other major finding: Global complexity is the foremost issue confronting these CEOs and their enterprises. The chief executives see a large gap between the level of complexity coming at them and their confidence that their enterprises are equipped to deal with it.

Until now creativity has generally been viewed as fuel for the engines of research or product development, not the essential leadership asset that must permeate an enterprise."

What Chief Executives Really Want:
http://finance.yahoo.com/news/pf_article_109596.html

Creativity – its Broader Value
Beyond the fact that it's an essential ingredient for successful, effective leadership, creativity can be the medicine for many conditions ailing corporations today. Here's a partial list:
> *Employee engagement*
> *Ownership and buy-in*
> *Enhanced collaboration*
> *Problem solving*
> *Embracing diversity and inclusion*
> *Process improvement*
> *Personal empowerment*
> *Self-esteem & confidence*
> *Increased happiness & work satisfaction*
> *Talent development*
> *Reducing stress*
> *Creating a benchmark for performance*
> *Facilitating change management*

In it's simplest form creativity is about generating ideas, generating something different – arranging old things in a new way; even if it's just a simple nuance or tweak.

Consider the evolution of toothpaste. In my workshop I ask, "In 10 seconds, list as many toothpaste options to purchase as possible." Here's some for starters:
> *…Mint*

…Standup packaging
…For children
…With mouthwash
…Baking soda
…Tarter control
…Whitening

And the list goes on. The powerful point here is that each of the choices is a tweak to the original – nothing daunting or earth shattering. And yet, each tweak or alteration no matter how slight has a proven revenue stream, all from one item.

In a broader sense, creativity is also about problem solving and enhancing critical thinking. **In essence, it's an all encompassing approach and experience in learning how to think effectively!**

Creativity asks of us to source for something outside our current framework. That whole "thinking outside the box thing" suggests this. It invites an approach to problem solving that asks us to go where you've probably not gone before (or at least forgot you've been) as suggested by Albert Einstein, "You cannot solve a problem at the same level of thinking at which you arrived at it."

In demystifying creativity then, we need to dismantle the misunderstandings generated around it so that it can be viewed and experienced in its purest form -- a simple act with a profound impact!

In fact, in order to address our corporate challenges of process improvement, developing a competitive edge, doing more with less, achieving new and better outcomes along with all the other ailments mentioned above, *creativity must be embedded in every work culture in a way that is approachable and practical.*

We must be able to help all stakeholders see that we all exhibit creative thinking in some way and then be trained on how to channel that capability into meaningful contexts for both corporate and professional success.

en·gage
/inˈgāj,enˈgāj/

verb
past tense: **engaged**; past participle: **engaged**

1. occupy, attract, or involve (someone's interest or attention).
   "he plowed on, trying to outline his plans and engage Sutton's attention"
   synonyms: capture, catch, arrest, grab, snag, draw, attract, gain, win, hold, gri
   captivate, engross, absorb, occupy
   "tasks that engage children's interest"
   antonyms: lose

   - cause someone to become involved in (a conversation or discussion).

Employee Engagement & Creativity – The Essential Power Couple

Employee engagement, at the time of this writing, is being seen as an "issue" and human resource buzz word. Solutions are being sought everywhere. Well…look no further, though not a cure-all, creativity definitely should be added to your employee engagement toolkit! Here's why.

As you begin to explore tapping and nurturing your creativity with the suggestions from this book, you'll notice something – the experience is very…well… engaging! Look at the list of descriptors in the definition provided for "engage." Yep, the process and action of being creative does all those and more.

Here is where I see employee engagement and creativity as an essential power couple. Employees who learn how to be creative, think innovatively, embrace strategic problem solving, discover that the very act of being creative is in itself an "engaging" experience.

Being creative is really more than an act, but an experience on a multi-sensory level; it is fun, exhilarating, intuitive, confidence building, surprising, relevant, collaborative, contemplative, motivating, spirited, bonding, accountable, fuels "work-esteem", at moments all encompassing and multi-dimensional. It nurtures a magnetic connection to desired outcomes as well as a commitment to the subsequent activity that can bring the resulting ideas to life!

In fact creativity can elevate how we see and nurture engagement. By its very nature it can achieve in this realm what other practices of engagement cannot. But alas, we must come down to earth and full circle to the current truths shared earlier regarding attitudes, lack of understanding and therefore lack of consideration for the value and role of creativity and innovative thinking in business operations.

Let's be honest, as a follow up to the CEO's survey referenced earlier regarding essential leadership qualities, this additional question needs to be asked, "How much is being invested in having a culture of creativity, innovation and diversity?" (I've added diversity because the more diverse a company culture is, the more creative it will be. I'll talk about that more in a later chapter).

Another way to frame the question, "Is there lots of lip service to this whole creativity thing?" My answer is unfortunately yes. For the record you can't have it – the culture, tools, practices, benefits, results -- unless you invest in it.

In my experience, it's claimed to be so needed; yet little is done to implement it in employee training or culture integration.

If we want employees to be more engaged, let's first start with leaders being more engaged in learning and experiencing their own creativity. And soon, these leaders will heartily welcome to their companies the power couple of creativity and engagement that they so desperately need and claim they want.

Employee engagement begins with leadership engagement.

Creativity – Your Change Management Ally

" 'The world hates change, yet it is the only thing that has brought progress."
- Charles F. Kettering

How many people like change? Not very many people I know! In general, we're wired to prefer routines. Our brains get good at doing the same old things and we quickly form habits – habits of thought and habits of behavior.

We drive the same way to work, we order the same foods from our favorite restaurants, and we perform basic tasks at work the same way each and every day. Consistency can be great – it has meaningful value. It provides security and safety and workable framework for us to exist. But, it can also suppress creativity.

Before we can unleash (and harness) our creativity, we have to warm up to the idea of change. In fact, we need to be able to not only change but *evolve*.

When you think of the word evolve, what typically comes to mind? For me, the word evolve brings about feelings of ongoing forward movement or perhaps a capability to adapt quickly to any new situation.

In my experience, I've found and determined that change can be a skill and a much-needed skill in our economy.

Here is another great challenge for leadership today – enabling your staff to become skilled at change. If we position them to understand and embrace change, and to have the tools to leverage it, while continuing to provide a compelling vision, we won't just survive change but we'll be able to *thrive* on change.

What Role Does Creativity Play in Change Management?

Let's revisit the previous paragraph where it references "providing a compelling vision." Vision is seeing, vision in fact is using the imagination to see something in a different way. Without leadership crafting and communicating that for employees during any kind of change, guess what they'll do? Create their own picture/vision of the future usually infused with a generous supply fear.

F antasized

E vents

A ppearing

R eal

Enabling and utilizing the ability to be creative is one of the greatest resources and partners to change. **The very act of initiating the process of creativity unlocks current, fixed thinking and invites and suggests change** -- initially in how things are seen. It generates a variety of views, presents new possibilities offering the option that all is not lost. There is hope.

Creativity generates hope. It offers profound value.

Any change, which is altering your current state to new results, begins with a new way of thinking and feeling that results in different decisions that produce different behaviors.

In fact, in order to thrive on change we've got to be able to change our perspective. Here's an example:

One day, a man by the name of Bill Bowerman was sitting at breakfast. His wife served him up an incredible, aromatic waffle. As Bill began to eat his waffle, he noticed that there were lines going every which way on his waffle. He thought "Hmm.." as he looked at those lines, all of the sudden something occurred to him. Bill thought "Could I take the design of this waffle and put it on the bottom of a running show?" He chewed, and he thought, chewed some more, and said to himself "I bet it could cushion the foot while creating more traction… Yeah, that's it!" He got up from the table, grabbed his wife's waffle iron, and utterly ruined it in the process making a prototype of the cushion for the bottom of a shoe.

No matter, Bill made more than enough money to buy his wife a new waffle iron. Bill's story is the story of one of the co-founders of Nike. His life was changed forever in part because of that one idea. All because one day he saw the lines of his waffles a little different. That one change of perspective, led to a creative solution to a problem he'd been wrestling with – how to improve the tennis shoe.

Every day we have the opportunity to see things differently, whether its new products or services, changing careers, or family challenges.

If you want different, you have to see different. If you want to see different you have to think different and that is the origin of the creative process.

Creative thinking is inherently connected to change. Why not leverage it? When we can get ourselves and others on-board with change by way of the creative process, all can thrive, fear can be minimized, positive expectations can be generated and new possibilities, process improvements, and so much more can be discovered.

"In this new world, wealth creation is dependent upon the capacity of a nation to continually create ideas."
- Phil McKinney

Read: http://philmckinney.com/archives/2010/02/ready-to-compete-in-the-creative-economy.html

Notes - Doodle Your Thoughts

We are visual creatures. When you doodle an image that captures the essence of an idea, you not only remember it, but you also help other people understand and act on it - which is generally the point of meetings in the first place.

Tom Wujec

ACT II
Welcome to the Gateway of Your Talent

You're capable of building a blazing fire.

| Step Through The Portal – Your Creative Self is Waiting

"Companies don't innovate – people do."
– Jeff Hawkins, creator of the Palm Pilot

Welcome to a gateway…a gateway into a new way of living, seeing and experiencing the world -- a gateway that will serve you and enhance your life both personally and professionally while boosting your own talent management.

The key to benefiting from this gateway is your willingness to enter it and once inside, commit to doing all that is asked of you.

My belief is nothing matters more than finding, acknowledging and living out your place in the world. Once inside the gateway, all that you experience will assist you in doing just that.

Though you may think this book is about creativity…and it is. it's more about you developing your capabilities, unlocking and nurturing your talent. That's the immense value creativity brings.

You see, I've discovered that creativity is a powerful resource for many things. It's a confidence builder, healer, stress reducer, inspirer, economic stimulator, change facilitator and relationship builder, to name a few. It can build a bridge between two shores while building a bridge between two hearts.

It's all about connecting…dots, thoughts, ideas, information, people, subjects, imagination, materials, all in the service of advancing the human community.

It's way more than learning how to draw or paint pretty pictures. It spans all educational disciplines (though many may not see it) and can enliven every part of the human experience.

It is us, who we are, how we got here, what we do, how we live.

I see you standing at the gateway as we speak. But before you enter, I have to ask this question, "Are you on lock down?"

Many people I know are on lock down.

I discovered this when conducting creative and innovative thinking workshops through-out North America. For some 15 years, workshop after workshop, I discovered how most people are not only on lock down, *many are shut down*— emotionally, mentally, spiritually and even physically.

My findings: The most unique and interesting parts of ourselves, where the essence of talent resides, is on lock down.

Working with creativity serves to "loosen" people up, to unlock what's been locked up—for years, probably since childhood. That's when the jail cell door had not yet been closed, but started to. And for many, the key was thrown away.

Creativity helps people find the key, unlock the cell and gently, safely coax themselves out—freeing the essence of their uniqueness to blossom into full uninhibited expression like a flower softly unfolding as it's enveloped in soothing, nurturing rays of sunlight.

Creativity helps people free themselves from lock down. Lock down is a pervasive syndrome in our society.

In my work, I've discovered the primary reason for lock down is fear of disapproval, because for many the core of who they are is so dissimilar to their surroundings and therefore not good, useful or needed. At least, that's what they've been conditioned to believe.

You see, it all began when you where young...when you started to become aware of yourself in relation to the people around you—and they became aware of you.

In the beginning, you were....well ...you.

But people began reacting and responding to you—giving you information about yourself *in relation to them.* Whatever information you received—you received and with nothing to compare it to, you took it as only you could—truth... and not knowing any better... it *became* your truth.

Life continued to happen and all experiences were filtered through that truth...and you adjusted accordingly. Those adjustments continued to lock you into place and that became the you—the you presented to the world.

Not necessarily the "inside you" mind you, but the *approved,* adjusted you. The you that conformed to those early accepted truths -- whether they were true or not. The lock down had begun...and it continued.

Until one day you sat in a class or a meeting and you were asked to express yourself—to have a voice, to share your perspective, to make an authentic and original statement. "Come on," someone encouragingly prodded, "we need some creative ideas—we need *your* creative ideas."

If you were in my workshop, that would be me advocating for your release, hoping to free you from years of confinement knowing that I don't have the key, but helping you *find your key.* You see, you've had it all along.

Consider this book serving that same role. This book is written in service to freeing your spirit, heart, intellect and talent.

Here is my message—unlock yourself. "With what key?", you ask, the key of self-acceptance—all of yourself, exactly yourself. We all are on a journey of self-acceptance and self-discovery—whether we're aware of it or not. Life presents us this free opportunity. Are we using it?

On the one hand we say, "Be different, we need different, we celebrate different, we're desperate for different. Different will make us more money, will solve our problems, cure our human ills."

> Here's the dilemma. That journey intersects with both the compelling need for creative and innovative thinking and our personal and societal struggle with differences and diversity.

On the other hand, we think and feel, "Wait a minute, your different is making me feel uncomfortable. Your different is strange to me. I'm not sure we want *your* different. I prefer comfort over different. Can you be sorta different, but still be mostly like us?"

In essence what they really want…is for you to stay on lock down. But you say, "Oh no I won't!"

I say give them what they need—they need the fully free, real you —though they may not know it and for many they don't.

Don't let them stop you! You grab that key, unlock your cell, discover and dust off the barely recognizable parts of you and begin to tune in, so you can turn on and tune up all that talent, so that ultimately you can turn out all of you and the best of you!

"Free at last, free at last, thank God almighty, you're free at last." Now that is true talent management!

"As long as you are creative, you have the power to express yourself as a free individual"

SIDEBAR | Lip Service or Leadership?

"In business, a creative idea is only worth as much as the manager who can recognize it." – Eric Jaffee

If you're reading this you may be an individual contributor or leader by title. I see a special responsibility for those who are official leaders regarding creativity. Are you contributing to the lock down of yourself and those you lead?

What does your leadership reflect regarding inviting ideas and diversity of thought? Do you give mixed messages in this area – that is… invite creative thought in one breathe and quickly knock it down, discouraging it in the next?

This is a compelling issue. I recommend you take the time to assess the culture of your team, department and company. Here are a few questions for starters:

- Is independent thinking encouraged?
- Do team members feel comfortable challenging the status quo?
- Is respecting differences a clear expectation within your team culture?
- Is there an atmosphere of respectful dialogue even with conflicting views?
- Do team members display a sense of confidence in their contribution?
- Do strong personalities dominant to the point that other team members refrain from participating and feel like "what's the point?"

Numbers Tell The Story
Linda Naiman, Creativity at Work Newsletter
Genius Level Creativity

In 1968, George Land distributed among 1,600 5 year olds a creativity test used by NASA to select innovative engineers and scientists. He re-tested the same children 10 years of age, and again at 15 years of age.

Test results amongst 5 year olds; 98%
Test results amongst 10 year olds; 30%
Test results amongst 15 year olds; 12%

Same test give to 280,000 adults: 2%

"What we have concluded," wrote Land, "is that non-creative behavior is learned."

Source: Escape from the Maze: Increasing Individual & Group Creativity, James Higgins | Breaking Point and Beyond, George Land and Beth Jarman, San Francisco, Harper Business, 1993

Creativity Is Simple and Common

You may have determined from reading so far that there is just a tremendous amount of confusion surrounding creativity. If we're going to embrace it and be it, we've got to know what it is. Though I've described it in a variety of ways, let's bring clarity to what it is:

Creativity can be defined in these simple terms...
> the state or quality of being creative.

>the ability to transcend traditional ideas, rules, patterns, relationships, or the like

>and to create meaningful new ideas, forms, methods, interpretations

Source: Dictionary.com Unabridged
Based on the Random House Dictionary, © Random House, Inc. 2015.

Additionally:
- ➤ Arranging old things in a new way
- ➤ Imaginative – having or showing imagination
- ➤ Originate
- ➤ Characterized by sophisticated bending of the rules or co nventions

Here's what I finding interesting about those descriptors, they are so common and simple. In fact, if we really looked for it, we could find them in our everyday lives in a variety of ways done by...well, just about anybody!

A panhandler concocts a different approach to solicit money.
A child figures a way to get something from his parents.
A spouse devises a way to conceal something from their partner.
A cook decides to try a new combination of ingredients.
A cashier discovers a way to apply an additional credit.
A teenager develops a scheme to miss school.

Think of the many basic day-to-day experiences in which you have said or thought to yourself, "Well that was creative." I call that list and those experiences "unintentional creativity."

It's creativity when we're not looking or intending it – we're just livin' life, doing what we do and then pop, an exercise of creative action solves a dilemma or achieves a different outcome.

We regularly have acts of random creativeness – we just may not notice it. Creativeness is embedded in how we live and navigate life and we learned to use it at a very early age.

This is what I call "the big disconnect." **Creativity is held at arms length while being such a natural part of how we live.** The very people who shy away from it are the very people who regularly demonstrate creativity without realizing it. This disconnect reflects how misunderstood it really is.

Exercise
Recognize and document acts of random creativeness
Sources to begin: family, co-workers

Intentional Creativity – The Ideation Process

"Ideas are knocking at my door 24 hours a day."
- Lou Reed, Rock Icon

What I have found to be so extraordinary about creativity is how multi-faceted it is. It can be both ethereal and practical. The intention of this book is to present it's multiple facets as if you're looking into a kaleidoscope viewing the array of colorful design. This chapter introduces the foundation of that.

For this section I recommend, having Crayola crayons and blank paper by your side.

There can be a practical process to being creative in the endeavor of generating ideas. Here are the tools and foundation for that process:
- ✓ Having a process format
- ✓ being aware of how the mind works on the simplest level
- ✓ belief
- ✓ and commitment

Consider these the starter "tinder" to igniting your fire of ideas.

First let's start with the definition of ideate. Look how astoundingly simple it is. We've all done each of these!
Ideate: to form an idea, imagine, conceive

The key to generating ideas, to having a steady flame of ideas is to create emotional, psychological and physical states and situations where ideation can *intentionally* happen. Know this – feeling intense negative stress is not the best emotional and physiological state to generate ideas.

In my workshop, when we begin working with the ideation process, we first get attendees to "loosen up" and stimulate the senses by introducing the process in a memorable, "child like" way...we shout and pound.

The ideation process goes like this...

Do it right now...
With your hands on your desk -
Chant and pound
Left...right...right...left
(left hand, right hand, right hand, left hand)

Do it again
Chant and pound
Left...right...right...left

What's the ideation process?
Left...right...right...left

Ah hah – you got it!

This is an interactive introduction to the creative process, which invites attendees to access their first grader – to connect with the time in their lives when creativity and play were as natural as breathing.

It was a time when we freely expressed ourselves, unedited – giving full force to our voice and energy. I invite you today, go back to being a first grader for the moment – to the simple, child like (vs. childish) expressive, uninhibited behavior in which you found so much joy. It is in replicating that space and context that you'll begin to unlock and tap your creative capability. Grab your paper and crayons. Put on your first grader hat. Pick up a crayon, smell it, remember the smell of Crayola crayons? Remember the feel and texture of holding a crayon? (By the way, Crayola crayons have a patented scent). Put that crayon in your opposite hand and write your first and last name when you were in first grade.

Does that somewhat resemble your first grade signature? For many it does!

Next, take a moment, using your imagination recall activities you did in play as a kid. Give yourself permission to daydream. Recall the sounds of laughter, the feeling of fun, companionship and uninhibited freedom of expression. (My acronym for fun is "fabulous, uninhibited, nonsense.")

As the play activities come to you, write them on your paper using the crayon and your opposite hand. Feel free to write the activities randomly -- all over the page. This exercise should stimulate a positive, uplifting and open sensory experience – you're starting to unlock. In fact every part of you should begin to unlock **especially your imagination**.

Note: With the sensation of unlocking, may also come the feeling of resistance.

You see, as children we primarily lived out of our imagination. We used things around us to

> *The true sign of intelligence is not knowledge but imagination.*
> *- Albert Einstein*

construct forts, concoct fake food, pretend we were soldiers or cowboys, teach and sing to now one, create fashion shows with

Barbies. Look at your activities list. Many of those were done with your imagination.

Our imagination was a childhood partner, our constant, loyal companion. It served us well. It allowed us to be all of what we could and wanted with no judgment (though some of us got into trouble for sure!) From our head to our toes, we were fully expressed! Oh the fun and joy of it!

Then as we grew up and began integrating into society, our lives became more real and less imaginative.

The ideation process, this journey and why I call it the gateway to your talent is all about recapturing and reconnecting with that loyal companion.

Your imagination is the portal to your individual freedom, unique expression and soulful voice.

Continuing the Ideation Process
Let's return to the ideation process of left, right, right, left. It's not only a fun approach to the ideation process but instructions on how to work the brain – the whole brain. This is a technique for strategically and intentionally managing key brain functions, which includes conscious and subconscious, right and left hemispheres for specific outcomes.

Again, as mentioned before, this is the practical side of creativity. It also leverages a little know fact that you can instruct your brain how to work. It's a nimble muscle that can be exercised as well as accessed. Knowing how it functions in its simplest forms is a must in maximizing the creative and well as critical thinking experience.

Please note as we go through these: we all have these functions. The brain all works together. However, there are functions and attributes attributed to certain sides that tend to be more dominant depending on the context.

Let's look at these key functions:

Left brain – logical, analytical, objective, judgmental, reasoning, linear, need for control, process, order, convergent and need to be right.

Right brain - intuitive, thoughtful, subjective, open, emotional, spontaneous, tangent, imaginative, divergent, big picture, visionary.

Conscious mind - consists of everything inside of our awareness. This is the aspect of our mental processing that we can think and talk about in a rational way.

Preconscious - part of the mind that corresponds to ordinary memory. These memories are not conscious, but we can retrieve them to conscious awareness at any time.

Subconscious - s a reservoir of feelings, thoughts, urges, and memories that are outside of our conscious awareness; deeply stored memories. (Some also use the word unconscious).

All of these brain functions are partners in thinking effectively and holistically. This encompasses creative, critical and innovative thinking. What the ideation process does is work with all of these in the most advantageous ways, ensuring each is used to its greatest capacity.

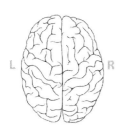

Now, with this brief introduction to key brain

functions, you'll appreciate and understand the ideation process and why it's designed the way it is.

Let's now work through what each segment of the ideation process means and why.

Left: Tell the left brain to shut up!...go to sleep don't need you right now. (You can also call it silencing or quieting it activity.)

Why?...because it will tend to judge, try to make sense of or logic away any ideas before they even have a chance of getting out of your mouth.

In fact, you might have messages to yourself (self talk) that discourage you from revealing anything that doesn't "sound" sane, logical or meet with others approval. If any inventor had listened to that kind of thinking, most of what we enjoy today, would not exist.

Right: Stimulate to activate the imagination
This is *the* essential piece to creativity that most don't realize needs to occur. Ever been in a meeting when someone says, "Ok, let's come up with ideas" and every sits there looking like a "deer in headlights"? Based on what you've learned so far...why? What's really happening is folks are being asked to generate ideas from left-brain thinking (or functions), without activating the imagination!

The key to successful creative thinking is rigorous activation and cultivation of the imagination.

Disney called it "imagineering." In fact the term was first introduced in the 1940s by Alcoa to describe its blending of imagination and engineering. It was adopted by Disney to identify the division of the company that designed and constructed theme parks.
http://en.wikipedia.org/wiki/Walt_Disney_Imagineering

I consider *stimulating the primer before the paint*. It prepares the brain for the more practical element of the ideation process.

Here are some of my favorite ways to quickly stimulate the right brain all in the spirit of waking it up and activating the imagination:

- Read children's books – many have bright, primary colors
- Draw on blank paper with crayons
- Sing
- Listen to music with your eyes closed
- Go on a brisk 5 minute walk
- Recall a favorite childhood play activity or memory and daydream
- Watch a cartoon – something particularly illogical
- Doodle
- Draw with your eyes closed (this is so fun!)

 Creative activity is a great way to reduce stress!

Saturate: Take in new information – soak your brain.
This is the more strategic and intentional part of the ideation process. It's the part that guides the brain to the outcomes

you're looking for.

When you hear the word saturate what comes to mind? I ask that question in every workshop and on one occasion an attendee said, "Fat." That brought a few laughs.

Here's another way to view it. Imagine for a moment, plunging a sponge into a bucket of water. When lifting it, it's heavy, completely soaked and dripping. This is what we mean by saturate.

So how do you saturate? If you want to generate new ideas, process improve, problem solve you need to consume a variety of new and relevant information for a period to time. Depending on the project or intent, at minimum 3-4 days. In fact soak your brain with complimentary information from what other companies are doing, best practices, what similar or parallel industries are doing around the topic or theme you are problem solving or ideating.

Saturation can also be compared to that of an actor preparing for a role. To do their best in playing a particular character, they will research, study, interview, in essence *immerse* themselves in every aspect of that character so that they can fully encompass the essence of the role. Some do it so well, you don't even recognize the actor no matter how famous. For many, they become transformed!

That immersion is an example of the principle of saturation. Saturation forces all aspects of your brain to *synthesize the new with the old.* Combining is a function of the creative process. And that's a really cool part of the creative process and how the brain works – your brain is working even when you're not!

Here's the key – if you don't give it anything new to combine with the old, you're basically churning the old into more old! This reminds me of the popular definition of insanity – doing the same things over and over again but expecting different results.

This part of the process speaks to one of my favorite quotes from Einstein referenced earlier, but bears repeating: "You cannot solve a problem at the same level of thinking at which you arrive at it." This is a common practice. Kind of insane really.

Creative Thinking Insight:
Diversity of knowledge is key to increasing your creative thinking. The more you know, the better resource your knowledge can be to source for new ideas – there is more to combine. An attendee in a recent class called it "cross pollinating"… well said!

And what you come up with may surprise you! I was recently conducting a management training seminar in which we were discussing the benefits of coach. One benefit offered was that of team synergy, chemistry or cohesion. This group had several words to describe a team having high productivity via good morale. All of sudden (this is an example of the brilliance of your subconscious) I gave an example that even surprised me. I liken the positive energy of a team fueling the productivity of its members to that of "drafting" in NASCAR (using the car in front of you to enable your car to go faster).

This particularly surprised me because at one time I neither liked nor understood NASCAR and now I'm using elements of it for management training.

One other note, related to creative thought and combining. During this same time, I had been teaching and talking a lot about using metaphors as a more effective form of explaining a concept or making a point. I truly believe those discussions combined with watching a race the Sunday before that training day created a "combinatory opportunity!" And the cool part was I wasn't consciously thinking, "Hum…what example can I use to drive home the point of team synergy?" The example just came out!

Source of drafting in the history of stock car racing:
Junior Johnson went from narrow escapes from the feds to narrow escapes from fellow stock-car racers. He noticed that whenever he got right behind another car, he was able to go faster. He suspected the front car lowered wind resistance for the back car by "creating a situation, a slipstream kind of thing." His technique helped him win the 1960 Daytona 500, even though his car was slower than some other cars on the track [source: Tierney].
http://auto.howstuffworks.com/auto-racing/nascar/nascar-basics/stock-car-racing-techniques1.htm

---

Let The Magic Begin!
Once you saturate your brain – let it all go! In fact stop thinking about the problem, issue or theme you've been thinking about. Have you ever heard of the phrase, "the way to solve a problem is not to think about it?"

Incubate
>to maintain at a favorable temperature and in other conditions promoting development
>to develop or cause to
develop gradually

The reality is you really are thinking about it... just not on a conscious level, in the traditional way you're use to. **Your subconscious will do the work for you – so you really can let it go.** You must trust the brilliance and design of how your brain works! Don't force the ideas. The more you trust, the more you'll allow it to fully do it's work – function at its best potential. Let it show you its power – your power. Allow yourself to enter into superpower mode! Just relax and look for the results.

In fact, if you don't it could hinder the deeper, better thinking, the brewing, the combining and synthesizing you want to take place. Your conscious thinking could very well drown out and squash the brilliance preparing to burst onto the scene.

This is considered the incubation state and the duration needed for certain outcomes is unpredictable. But one thing for sure, ideas will start popping out without you having to "think" about them!

And it may go from popping to bursting as they reveal themselves in the most unlikely ways and places. I call it the 3 "Bs' of the incubation state: *bed, bath and busy!*

Do you...
- Ever get an idea in the shower (or bathroom in general)?
- Ever get clarity on an issue when you're just waking up in the morning? (That's where the phrase let me sleep on it comes from – your subconscious mind is working it out with your deepest self).
- Ever get an idea when you're exercising, running or doing mundane chores or activities?
- Ever get ideas when you're driving?

News flash! Your best ideas typically do not come to you at work or in a stressed state, but when you're relaxed and your thinking mind (conscious mind) is not fully functioning!

This truly is the fun part. Here's where you get to witness what your brain is capable of when instructed and used with intention. You will surprise yourself and be very pleased with the possibilities presented to you! And that's exactly what you want – lots of possibilities, options and ideas.

The intention in using the ideation process is to generate lots of ideas rather than trying to come up with the best ideas first, which in many cases ends up being just a few.

I've discovered in this work most people have taken on the notion that to effectively generate ideas, you need to come up with the best ideas first and 2 or 3 will do. But what does that do to the creative process? It stifles and constricts it, and could ultimately shut it down.

We've come to realize that it's not idea 1, 2 or 3 that's the best but usually idea 13 or 20 or in many cases a combination thereof. It ends up being various acts of combining or rearranging of multiple options that then generates the best idea or the most relevant idea at the moment.

This is not to say that the first idea, spark or inspired idea is not the one. It may very well be. The *ideation process,* however, has a different intention and expected outcomes.

With this in mind, it's imperative that you capture your ideas as often as you can even if they don't make sense or seem relevant at the moment. Consider your ideas your intellectual gold that you may be able to redeem some day! Treat them with respect.

Important Tip: Have an idea file. When you get one, put it in there. Don't edit or judge. See it as valuable even if it's not relevant at the moment.

Respecting your ideas is a way of respecting yourself, your gifts and talents.

Essential Saturation Comrades

It's at this point in my workshops that I stop to highlight two important aspects of the saturation stage:
1. Generating volumes of ideas
2. Getting intentional outcomes

Those aspects have 2 critical comrades -- the words HOW and LOTS.

I can't emphasize enough that the power of the ideation process is for the purpose of initially and continually generating LOTS of ideas as well as a "key spark." Its not about getting just "an idea" or solving "a problem." Though ultimately that will happen. If you start from that alone, you will constrict the process and limit the better outcomes. Again, this is the place to amplify the process to excavate the most ideas possible.

Here's an example. In our last section we'll be talking about tools for generating ideas. Two exercises attendees of my workshop experience are mind dumping and mind mapping. We do both with very random elements.

After those two activities are complete, I ask them to create something practical from the results; for example a welcome party for a new team member or and marketing campaign for a new product.

The outcomes from that experience are amazing, hilarious and very surprising! Attendees are amazed at what they developed from random sets of words, phrases and concepts without ever having the end in mind.

This is not to say this is the only way it should be done. I'm suggesting that this is a method rarely used or considered and from which amazing results can be achieved. It is truly a way of expanding options. It's probable that in this case having the end in mind, would limit the creative, random possibilities because the left brain would be activated to edit in the spirit of it "needing to fit."

Having the end in mind for a more experienced "ideator" is an effective approach. The experienced ideator has been trained to not limit or constrict the process. They recognize when process perils can occur and have learned how to effectively manage them.

Special note: (I know I'm repeating myself here.) Though our goal is to generate lots of ideas and options, as with anything this is not absolute. This doesn't mean the first or second idea would not be the best one to go with or test. Here is where instinct, intuition and belief come in. Your gut can say, "This is the one," and it might well be the one! And this is the glory of creativity and what makes it so much fun! There is not one fixed rule for everything; there is great variety in approaches and tools to achieve the desired outcome(s).

The purpose of lots of ideas is to help those new to the creative process learn how to cultivate and <u>expand their capacity to think</u>. Generating a few ideas could be nothing more than lazy thinking – consider Martin Luther Jr.'s earlier quote. My experience is that in general people tend to think from a puddle vs. learning how to think from reservoir.

This quote is a great lead into the second aspect and second comrade of the saturation stage: generating intentional outcomes.

The other comrade during the saturation and incubation period is the power of asking with the word "how."

I've mentioned several times the exciting notion that you can instruct your brain how to work. This is easily achieved in using the word "how". It is a mind-blowing and fun experience in generating ideas for a specific need or outcome.

Simply put, when you ask yourself a question, your brain goes to work to answer it for you. Consider it the Google Ask or Siri of the ideation and problem solving process. Their function is to search and source from the vast information bank of the internet to provide your answer. Your subconscious asks in a similar fashion (and this is where diversity of knowledge plays its part). The best time to do this is right before you go to sleep so you can leverage the essential brain activity while you sleep, including dreaming.

Years ago I use to travel with a dear speaker colleague Candy Whirley. We conducted creativity day camps for corporate trainers throughout the country. One thing about Candy, she loved color and balloons. We'd use those balloons for the opening session and they'd subsequently beautify the seminar room for the rest of the day with no other use.

One day it occurred to me that we certainly could be using them for other activities. So, during our travel week, throughout the day and each night, I asked myself, "How else can we use these balloons?"

Two days past and the next morning in the shower, a movie appeared in my head (with no prompting) that showed people writing on balloons, people batting the balloons while music was playing, the music would stop, they would grab the balloons and read what was written. The music would begin again as well as the batting of the balloons.

This turned out to be an activity called "batting around an idea" for ending the workshop. Attendees would write a few ideas, takeaways or review points on the balloons. We would turn on music and they would bat them around the room. When the music stopped, they would grab the nearest balloon and read the information written. This would be repeated several times. This was a great interactive review.

I firmly believe I would not have come up with that idea, had I not **intentionally** asked for a solution using the *power of how.*

Incubation & The Inspired Spark
Once your brain has been primed during the saturation, incubation period, be prepared for ideas to pop up in the oddest ways as your brain continually attempts to problem solve or naturally combine even without expressed intention or prompting such as the NASCAR example.

Along with the "3 bs", bed, bath, and busy, events or moments of inspiration will provide ideas as well. Our previous story of Bill Bowerman seeing a waffle as a cushion for an athletic shoe is a great example of inspired problem solving or the "inspired spark."

Another great example is the title of this book. I had a few in mind, polled friends, colleagues and family members and had settled on this one: You are the solution - How to unleash your creative powers. I thought it was a solid, good title. Then…the inspired happened!

I went looking for art for the book and came across this:

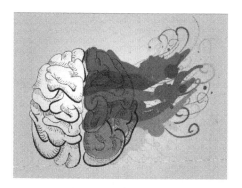

I immediately connected to it on an energetic level – it hit me! It felt so compelling, dramatic and reflected the boldest points I wanted to express. Seeing it in color had a magnetic affect.

My initial thought, "Wow, it looks like a brain on fire. That's how lit up I want the right brain and imagination to be for ideation!" It inspired my thinking…my brain starting connecting that metaphor to what I was writing and from that moment I decided to change the title of the book with no hesitation, convinced this was the art work and concept I wanted to work with. It also inspired the preface and the broader description and messages I wanted to convey –> brain on fire = creating/thinking superpowers!

And finally, the last piece of the ideation process

Left: Tell your left-brain to wake up!
By now it's lonely, it feels as if it's been on vacation too long. It wants to go to work. Now's the time to intentionally engage the conscious mind -- those left brain functions...and what will it happily do? It will start sorting through your ideas, trying to make sense of them, seeing what fits, judging their relevance.

And that's all good with a word of caution. Be keenly aware of two functions, albeit enemies that could quickly sabotage all your hard work.

They are: fear & limiting / sabotaging beliefs

FEAR
Be careful; don't let the left-brain kill your ideas. Please be aware that if you are not familiar or comfortable with using your ideas or putting them out there, your left-brain functions may over judge, or squash them out of fear!

Presenting new ideas makes you vulnerable; they expose you to potential ridicule. The naysayers will start swarming around them like mosquitos to skin on a hot, sweltering day and then suck the life right out of them.

As you begin to nurture your intellectual capital and talent, which is what cultivating creative thinking is, you must be willing to unhook yourself from the need for approval.

When you put forth ideas you are saying, "See, here's something to consider that will change our current situation." At that point, in that moment, YOU become the leader – official title or not and you are suggesting change! **Not only is your idea out front, YOU are as well.**

This is where you have to commit to not letting your job title dictate your talent! Leadership is not necessarily a title -- it is a behavior.

In that moment *you are the thought leader.* You have committed to being a shepherd and responsible steward of the gift that idea or subsequent ideas will bring for the greater good!

> Do not give in to fear!
> Fear is one of the greatest enemies of human potential
> and of *your* talent and progress in the world.

Limiting and Sabotaging Beliefs
Beliefs are the carpet on which your ideas will ride to their new destination or die where conceived. They won't get anywhere without them. With supporting beliefs…even as simple as, "These ideas are worthy of testing," they'll have a chance of making it to the light of day.

Let's go back to the part where we discussed how the typical left brain functions might behave when an idea is initially conceived (and why we tell it to shut up at the beginning of the ideation process). Those functions, judge, edit and try to make sense of something quickly. It is not comfortable with risk. It needs to be right and in control. If an idea doesn't appeal to logic or presents too much "perceived" risk, it will easily and expeditiously eliminate it as an option to consider (thinking its doing you a great service by the way) – *before* its value has had a chance to be tested and proven.

In the attempts to judge and make sense of, a barrage of thoughts may come, which in general, fall into one of three categories (and here is where the fear is generated).

> Thoughts that are sabotaging beliefs.
Sabotage means it has no chance at all.
> *Examples:*
> "This definitely won't work."
> "That's a stupid idea."
> "People will think I'm crazy for bringing this up."
> "That makes no sense to me."

> Thoughts that are limiting beliefs
Limiting means its possible but untested, *predetermined constraints* are placed on how far or how much something can happen.
> *Examples:*
> (Here's one of my favorite) "640K ought to be enough for anybody." Bill Gates 1981
> "We'll only be able to use this in a few situations.
> "I think I'll only be able to get a few people on board with this project."
> "I'll never make more the X amount of money a year."

> Thoughts that are empowering beliefs
Empowering means "giving power to." Energy and attention is given, possibilities are considered and nurtured.

Examples:
"Let's see what's possible."
"This idea could really make a difference."
"This idea could present additional options to solve the problem."

Be Prepared For The Naysayers

When you're in the throws of flushing out your ideas I really want you to have these comments in your consciousness to encourage you at that moment of hesitation or doubt, and to remind you to manage your limiting and sabotaging beliefs.

Have in mind the following naysayers. You'll notice they all fall under the category of limiting or sabotaging beliefs.

Did they really say...

"Computers in the future may weigh no more than 1.5 tons." -- Popular Mechanics forecasting the relentless march of science, 1949

"I think there is a world market for maybe five computers." -- Thomas Watson Chairman of IBM 1943

"There is no reason anyone would want a computer in their home." --Ken Olsen president, chairman and founder of Digital Equipment Corporation, 1977

"This 'telephone' has too many shortcomings to be seriously considered as a means of communication. The device is in here late of no value to us." --Western Union internal memo 1876

"The concept is interesting and well formed, but in order to earn better than a 'C' the idea must be feasible. " --a Yale university management professor in response to Fred Smith's paper proposing reliable overnight delivery service processes. (Federal Express)

"Who the hell wants to hear actors talk?" --HM Warner, Warner Brothers 1927

"A cookie store is a bad idea. Besides the market research reports say America likes crispy cookies no soft and chewy cookies like you make." --response to Debbie Field's idea of starting Mrs. Fields Cookies.

"We don't like their sound, and guitar music is on the way out." --Decca Recording Company rejecting the Beatles, 1962

"If I had thought about it I wouldn't have done the experiment. The literature was full of examples that said you can't do this." --Spencer Silver on the work that led to the unique adhesive for 3M Post-it notes notepads.

Remember, don't initially expect people to see what you see. Its in your imagination, not theirs. Your job is to help them see, what you see. Seeing is the beginning of believing. At that moment – YOU are the thought leader, the vision leader!

"Without vision, the people perish."
- Proverbs 29:18

Setting The Stage

All of what we discussed so far can be greatly enhanced with one additional element. In order for the ideation process and experience to flourish at it's best, the optimum and proper conditions must be included.

It's spring at the time of this writing. It's a very exciting time as we prepare for planting a garden and look to see how the seeds that will blossom into a beautiful array of flowers we'll enjoy through-out the summer and into late fall.

I've learned over the years that getting the best yield in our garden, along with brilliant colors from our flowers has a lot to do with soil preparation. The conditions must be at their optimum for the best results. Many people assume that just because it's soil, it will do the job. I've discovered not all dirt has the best or appropriate nutrients to produce the optimum results. So, preparing it is key.

It's the same in "growing" ideas. Up until now we've talked about how to prepare the soil, the space where the seeds of ideas will originate and germinate, how the starting tinder should be arranged so the idea sparks have a chance to grow.

For the ideation process to be continually nurtured, like adding water, sunlight and additional fertilizer, the best conditions must be in place. What are those conditions? *Consider these four:*

- **Allow for it**
- **Plan for it**
- **Commit to it**
- **Believe in it**

Allowing for it and planning for it go hand in hand. Practically, here's what it looks like:

- → taking time
- → blocking out your schedule
- → discovering and visiting your most inspiring places
- → going to where inspiration and ideas can occur (not necessarily the same as the previous).

You could consider this the variety of wood and levels of oxygen needed to maintain the flame, reignite the embers or get that fire blazing!

Here's an example of the difference between the last two. For me being in nature is a place of calm and peace where I can hear myself and get rejuvenated -- giving space for things to percolate from within. New York is a place I go to get inspired— it's externally stimulating. The energy and diversity of people and buildings really stir me. Think of it as getting inspiration from within and from without.

Companies, for example, that recognize the importance of being in the best conditions, are aware of what that does and doesn't mean. What it doesn't mean is being at the office with relentless stress and unyielding deadlines. What it does mean is getting out, changing the immediate surroundings and respecting different ways and places people get inspired or generate ideas.

 Here are a few creative ways companies demonstrate their understanding and commitment to the creative capital of their employees:

___| Every seven years, designer Stefan Sagmeister closes his New York studio for a yearlong sabbatical to rejuvenate and refresh their creative outlook. The results was some very "inspired" results. See his Ted Talk: http://www.ted.com/talks/stefan_sagmeister_the_power_of_time_off

___| Google regularly gives engineers time away from their daily jobs to work on creative projects that are of personal, unique interest. Up to 20% of their work week can be applied to these projects. Believe it or not, one significant result of this practice, which they term "20% projects" – Gmail!

___| 3M predates Google with a similar practice (for 3M, it was 15%). The result of which was Art Fry accidently stumbling upon the lighter paper adhesive, which eventually became the post-it note.

___| Though not outside, yet a different environmental condition, Bill Gates' old office at Microsoft has been transformed into a "tinkering center" called "The Garage". It's filled with techno-toys, which employees can tinker with at their leisure. It's common practice for an entire team to spend a week in the "garage."

___| Eventbrite has a Zen Room at its office in San Francisco. Here employees can meditate, think or nap on soft, cozy couches. It's a low light, no noise environment.

Source: Read more: http://www.businessinsider.com/how-tech-companies-boost-creativity-2013-7?op=1#ixzz3WX531dBH

Conditions are the Fertilizer
At the beginning and through-out

Setting the stage or arranging the best conditions can <u>aid and substantially enhance</u> all four steps of the ideation process.

Consider these additional elements in maximizing every stage of the ideation experience and I invite you to add more! Ask yourself where might each of these fit best for you? At what step would you want to use them?

Exercise:
Map out the suggested elements into the ideation process in a way that would best support your creative undertaking:
Left – quiet the left brain
Right – stimulate your imagination
Right – saturate with relevant and new information
Left – wake up the left brain for evaluation of the ideas

- Detachment
- Quiet
- Nature
- Unclutter
- Exercise – movement, dance
- Eat natural vs. processed foods
- Practice unedited expression (music, writing (with paper and pencil/pen, crayons, markers, speaking, acting, improv)
- Have fun – play
- Have sensory experiences you're not use to (e.g. Play-Doh, finger paint, work with clay, drums, collages, legos, puzzles

What's Best For You?

Do you know? I ask that as final piece to this section. In many ways this whole creativity endeavor is about getting to know yourself better, what you're capable of, what works best for you. At this point in the process, you honestly may not know.

So, use this experience as a source of self-discovery. As mentioned earlier, the adventure of creativity is the gift that keeps on giving. It's very dimensional and generous in what it can offer.

I encourage you to identify your best *creative conditions*. Ask yourself what are the...

- ☑ Times of the day, week, calendar season?
- ☑ Spaces and places that inspire me, or stimulate my senses?
- ☑ Spaces and places that allow me to relax, detach and hear my inner voice and musings?
- ☑ Tools to use, whether it's a specific kind of writing utensil or paper, colors that I connect with?
- ☑ Means and conditions for self expression that help me "get it out". Is it alone or with others. Could it be with voice recording or videos?

The Creative Flow – Brain on Fire

All of the elements of the ideation process shared so far can be used with levels of volume, intention and intensity. Depending on your need and desire you can create a lite, simple flame or a blazing fire. It's all about time, attention, intention, conditions and materials.

As you're learning to tap and unleash your creativity, there is a possibility that you may not experience the level of superpower. Not there you're not capable, but because you may not be allowing.

For some this may sound odd, but I must say it. I believe and have experienced that the superpower level feels a bit spiritual, albeit inspired. For example – I can tell when I've written something that's ok, perhaps a bit cerebral and something that truly came from a different place.

A day later I'll go back and review it thinking, "Wow that's really good, where did that come from?"…and at that moment attempt to write in that way and I can't.

I've noticed that once I start a creative endeavor, it begins at a certain level. Then as I continue, I begin to relax and subsequently experience this feeling of letting go, like a sense of release.

Once that occurs, a greater flow of energy (in this case manifested as writing) takes place. The longer I stay in that state the more intense the flow…and the better ideas, concepts and insights transpire. It's as if the energy has been unleashed. The flow has now taken over and is in control of what's revealed on the page.

I've experienced that flow with significant intensity. My brain, my head was resonating so much energy, you could say it was energetically "on fire." It truly feels like a superpower!

Whatever you feel comfortable calling it: on fire, inspired, in the flow, in the zone (common in sports) it's a must to experience. It's an amazing sense of your potential, what you're capable of producing where you truly can surprise yourself. It is the place and state of your brilliance -- your genius at work!

"Wake-up your creative genius."
- Kurt Hanks

ACT III
Your Creative Thinking Toolkit

To build the flame and stoke its power, it's worth it to collect a variety of woods.

| Introduction - Your Creativity Toolkit

"If you only have a hammer, you tend to see every problem as a nail."
-Abraham Maslow

I love that quote! It truly represents the challenges in addressing and hopefully solving our most pressing issues.

To become a powerhouse thinker – to really get your brain on fire, you'll need tools for a variety of situations. Some will play the role of delicately arranging tinder; some will serve as the oxygen that sets the ideation process ablaze. Combined with the 4 conditions, you can successfully cultivate a robust creative and critical thinking capacity that can be accessed when needed.

In my workshop, after we work through the ideation process, we start to build the creative and critical thinking toolkit. You should have one. It includes a variety of ways (exercises) to jump-start the imagination, continually cultivate holistic thinking, nurture critical thinking, approaches to process improvement and problem solving.

In summary, the creativity toolkit includes anything that helps you in these areas.

> **Creative thinking**
>> ---- *having* or showing an ability to make new things or think of new ideas
>> ---- *using* the ability to make or think of new things : involving the process by which new ideas, stories, etc., are created
>> http://dictionary.reference.com/browse/creativity

> **Innovative thinking**

   ---- to introduce something new for or as if for the first time,
   ---- make changes in anything established

> **Critical thinking**

   ---- the intellectually disciplined process of actively and
   skillfully conceptualizing, applying, analyzing,
   synthesizing, and/or evaluating information gathered
   from, or generated by, observation, experience,
   reflection, reasoning, or communication, as a guide to
   belief and action. Source:
   http://www.criticalthinking.org/pages/defining-critical-thinking/766

Of note is the overlap in those definitions. The key themes of
focus are: new, make changes, process, and ability.

> To successfully and continuously fulfill all three of these
> definitions, you'll need a toolkit to do so. You'll have in
> your toolkit both tangible and intangible tools that partner
> with personal characteristics, coupled with the best
> conditions.

Up until this section, we've revealed the characteristics and
conditions that will help you maximize the tools such as
empowering beliefs and a strategic, intentional process.

In this section, tools will be presented that can be used alone
and with others and at any stage of the ideation process. They
will also be presented in broad categories – I don't want you to
get too boxed in when considering their use. Since I consider

this a workbook as well, I've left space for some writing and notes.

Your goal is to add to your toolkit sourced and ideated from this section.

Many suggestions can have a variety of approaches, which present exponential value! For those I'll say, "Now determine additional ways this can be used." Generating multiple variations, even of one exercise or activity is just more fun and is also an *essential part* of all three key terms mentioned above.

That essential part is *pushing limits whether created consciously or subconsciously*. It's knowing and believing there's more. Remember the statement -- thinking from a puddle vs. thinking from a reservoir.

As a reminder, you're first set of ideas, are just the warm up. True creative and critical thinking is not settling for the first phase of results, but understanding that multiple attempts with different approaches can achieve the better results. You must be willing to mine for those golden nuggets, not yet discovered.

Using Props

The final, tangible elements to your toolkit are props. I love using props in my workshops for a variety of topics. They are great companions to the creative exercises in your toolkit (as well as anchors in learning). The best thing about props is they can be found anywhere at anytime...really!

I'll share a few examples I've used in different topic areas or heard in my workshops *(many of these are presented in my Creativity Day Camp for Trainers & Presenters):*

Rubberband: team building and leadership session - What can a rubber band teach us about being a successful team member or provide clues to essential leadership qualities?

Qtip: customer service – acronym for quit, taking, it, personally; communication – two sides to every story.

Eraser: for learning something new – it's ok to make mistakes

Lifesavers: diversity; team members can be lifesavers | OSHA training for tips techniques (tied each color to a concept or rule)

A rock: (yes, you got it) A manager put a rock with a post it note on each team member's desk that read..."you rock."

General sources: candy, items from a craft store, items from a party store. I suggest in my Trainers Day Camp a field trip to Michael's Crafts, Hobby Lobby, Party City, to name a few, and do so through the lens of a trainer. Source tools and materials for the learning experience.

Recently I was conducting a Creativity Boot Camp for Trainers for a client in Virginia Beach. I like to go to the local office supply store to see if they carry anything unique or something standard that I can use differently.

I came upon a large desk calendar pad which sparked the idea to have each attendee *draw* what they learned from the day (or answer the question, "What were your key take-aways from the day?) on the desk calendar sheet. With crayons and a large sheet of paper went to work. What a fun way to end a creativity workshop (or any for that matter)!

GOT PROPS? *Prop ideas….*

Mental Preparation

As with stimulating the right brain or activating your imagination, there needs to be some pre ideation activity. *We loosen up to get unlocked.* We arrange the tinder before we lite the match. And the best way to do so is with mental exercises or "warm-ups." A variety of these should be in your toolkit.

In my workshops, many are conducted primarily in groups to leverage the energy and synergy for greater stimulation. But that's the beauty of any of this – there are not rules, discovering variations are part of the experience and challenge.

From a group perspective here are few of the benefits and results of "warm-ups."

- ☑ Increase blood flow to the brain
- ☑ Bonding with team members
- ☑ The feeling of fun - lots of laughter
- ☑ Increased self awareness, particularly in self editing
- ☑ An opening of the imagination
- ☑ Feeling a bit like a kid (in a good way)
- ☑ A dissipation of negative stress
- ☑ A sense of positivity
- ☑ Increased confidence in self expression

Primers

Primers can be described as exercising your mental muscle, disrupting routine, and challenging one-dimensional or one approach thinking. Here's a few to get you started

Read upside down

Drawing, with your eyes close
Do this with crayons in a variety of colors in front of you to grab randomly. Focus on the picture in your "minds eye."

Write your name backwards with your opposite hand

Puzzles

Perspectives - Noticing, fixed perspective

Riddles

Joke Writing

Metaphors, Analogies & Similes

Brain Teasers

Meditation

SCAMS
Build your fluency of thought and expression. Write 5 word sentences from the five given letters, one letter for each word.
S C A M S
Here are a couple of examples:
Senior citizens arrange maximum security.

Sarcastic comments are meant seriously.

How see how many sentences you can produce?
Variations

Lifestyle - Disrupting Routine.

Drive a different way to work

Brush your teeth with the opposite hand

Sleep on a different side of the bed

Write with your opposite hand for a period of time

Try a new activity you've never done before

Read a magazine on a topic of which you have no natural interest

Travel someplace new

Note: you can see the theme of "new" is prevalent here.

Add more….

Visual Challenges

Here's a popular one. How many squares are there? (This also can be done with a group.)

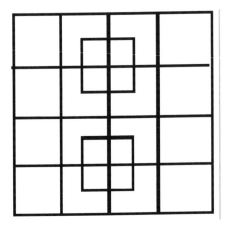

Certainly there is lots of variations on how to use this visual. Let's start with this one. Discover some abstract connection that links all the various diagrams in A and that distinguishes them from all the other diagrams in group B.

SPOT THE DIFFERENCES | Visual Discrimination Activities

Can you spot 20 differences between these pictures?

See this site for more; http://pixshark.com/visual-discrimination-activities.htm

This site has a lot of resources for visual memory, pattern identification, etc.

Thought Experiment

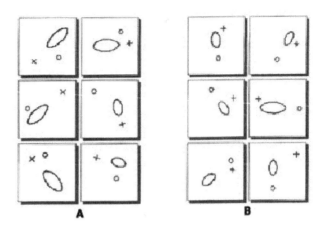

http://creativethinking.net/perception-and-pattern recognition/#sthash.BuTnfyJD.dpbs

For a more expanded explanation, go to the link provided. For the moment do this:

Instruction: Describe the differences between the set of pictures in Set A and the pictures in Set B. Answer is at the end of this chapter

Variation on this exercise:
- ➤ *Write a series of questions related to the above instructions.*
- ➤ *Describe the similarities and differences of each picture whether on side A or B.*
- ➤ *Do this as a group exercise. Pass a paper around to each team member, choose a variation to use, each adds one answer to the paper. This exercise is done in silence.*

Warm-ups

The A-Z Warm-up – 3 rounds, timed 30 seconds each

Round 1
Go through the alphabet naming women's names: each name starts with a letter of the alphabet. Each team member does one letter/name at a time starting with A. Each team member gets a turn until the team gets to Z. The goal is to get to Z within 30 seconds. For round 2 and 3 try to beat previous 'record."
Round 2
Repeat, this time using men's names.
Round 3
Back to women's names, but this time *make them up.*

Debrief: Ask, how many beat their record (many don't). Then ask, "In theory should round 3 have been the fastest?" Most respond, "yes." Then ask, "Well what happened. Why not?"

Round 3 should be the fastest but usually is the slowest. In asking why not, lots of interesting answers are revealed. The key answers are around self-editing… like didn't want to sound or appear stupid and adding rules where rules did not exist.

Make the point: Fear if the enemy of human potential, authentic expression and great ideas! Self-editing is usually an expression of fear.

This is a great exercise to develop self-awareness around self-editing. The important part to emphasize is that we put limits on our creative expression usually because of fear – fear of being embarrassed and vulnerable!

This is a great time to reinforce the point *to unhook ourselves from the need for approval* when participating in the ideation process and that in that moment when you put forth an idea, you are the leader. Committing to sharing ideas, being the "thought leader" is each participant's contribution to serving the good of the whole.

"Many great ideas have been lost because the people who had them could not stand being laughed at." --Unknown

Thinking In Pictures

This is an exercise that teaches how to generate pictures as a way of thinking. It's the imagination version of word association.

This is another "go around to each person' with speed, like the previous one. The point to this exercise is it will go faster when participants source their answers from the pictures they create when each category is called (rather than "left-brain" word association.)

State a category: for example "beach", each team member states an item in that category, then after about 30 seconds (you could even use a timer) switch to a new category, "grocery store", repeat. Other categories: school, football game, baseball game, park etc.

Variation: have team members write a category on an index card. Using a sand timer, every 30 seconds flip over to the next card. This is a good way to do it if there is one group and no facilitator. Otherwise with multiple groups, the facilitator is shouting out the next category.

Outcome: there should be an increase in how quickly team members shout out items because they are learning how to source from pictures – in essence thinking in pictures.

Category Alternative
Pick a category. Each team member states an item in that category, but that item needs to start with the last letter of previous item.
Example: Category – Grocery Store:
      First word (first team member) – tomato
      Second word (next team member) onions

Next team member: salt
Next team member: taco shells

Activating the imagination

Mind dumping

Uses of – for a fixed period of time take an object and record what it could be used for targeting a lot of variety -- try to be as illogical as you can: this can also be done in a group. My favorite item for this exercise is a cup (usually a drinking cup usually found at a hotel or at an event).

IBM holds what it calls "jams," which are massive brainstorming events focused on a specific topic.

The most famous jam is probably the one that took place in 2006 called the "Innovation Jam" - the largest IBM online brainstorming session ever held.

The company brought together more than 150,000 people from 104 countries and 67 companies and they came up with 10 new ideas that IBM invested $100 million into developing, including things like smart healthcare payment systems and a 3D Internet.

Read more: http://www.businessinsider.com/how-tech-companies-boost-creativity-2013-7?op=1#ixzz3WX4VUz7I

"Sometimes you need a vision so big...that to others it just sounds down right ridiculous ..."
– JoAnn Corley

Mind-mapping

Allowing unedited train of thought for a period time; can be done alone or in a group. (Though there is mind-mapping software on line, I feel the best way to do this is with pen/pencil on paper free form. For me, the mind mapping software feels somewhat mechanical and therefore "left-brain" ...more like categorizing than the expression of mapping, as if you're *creating a drawing*.

Source:
http://www.mindmapinspiration.co.uk/#/trymindmapping/453248
6456

Story Telling

Can be done… (lots of variations can be generated here.)

- ✓ verbally in a group
- ✓ alone in writing
- ✓ alone and then combine with a group

Approaches & Variations
(randomness is a key element here)

Have team members write phrases on an index card, then mix them up, layout in a certain arrangement and tell a story. Each participant contributes their part of the story sourced from the card they draw, or from the next card in the arrangement.

Have starter words on index cards that are mixed up, then put in and pulled from a bag.

In each case as the story is being told, a prop can be randomly introduced that needs to be incorporated.

A story can be told prompted by props pulled out of a bag every 30 seconds, a new prop is pulled for the next person to use or the entire group needs to incorporate it in some way (can use a sand timer).

One-story can be created around one prop, category or phrase starter. *Example:* "The broccoli said to the lettuce…"

✐ **How else can you "story tell"**

Expand your thinking with innovation suggestions.

Use the umbrella as your point of reference. How many options/idea can you generate under each of the 'scammperr" categories? This is one of those exercises that you can challenge yourself to push the limits of what you can produce.

It's also the kind of exercise where you can observe how people interpret the instructions of the exercise (fascinating!!). Therefore, if you're using these with multiple groups, it's important not to give too many instructions, but allow them to have the freedom to apply their own interpretation.

You'll notice for some participants they'll want you to give more instructions because they don't feel comfortable figuring it out for themselves, primarily due to the fear of being "wrong". The beauty of the ideation process, which is what they need to learn, is that there is no right or wrong, just different.

Variation: Do this type of exercise over a period of time, e.g. a week, or a month. Do it with others for a set duration. Create a huge group mind-map.

Combine   Adapt   Modify

Substitute   SCAMMPERR   Magnify

Reverse   Put to other uses

Rearrange   Eliminate

Creative & critical thinking... through the power of questions

You may recall as we were working through the ideation process that using the word "how" was a key companion.

In general, asking questions is a substantial tool and skill in expanding how we see or examine a situation and source for ideas leading to solutions. It expands possibilities and understanding. I call the words used to do this -- "the power 6":

who, what, when, where, how, and why.

A really fun exercise in my workshop to experience this is done by posing this question: **If all cars where yellow?....** The attendees are challenged to use each of the power 6 in exploring this question. It's a great way to learn to think more critically and dimensionally.

This is also a wonderful exercise to do over a period of time as an individual or with a team. The challenge is to revisit each category adding more questions to each, particularly when you're able to sleep on it for a period of a week or longer.

Start with 3-5 items for each word...

Who

What

When

Where

How

Why

Day Dreaming

One of the most famous advertising campaigns was envisioned on a walk to the deli. After days of brainstorming, Creative Director Eric David repeated "Aflac-Aflac-Aflac" in his head on a walk to grab lunch when he had the "aha!" moment. David returned to the office with his sandwich, quacking "Aflac" at his team. He created one of the most well known ducks in the advertising world while daydreaming on his lunch break.

Of all the problem solving activities, daydreaming allows you to be the most open-minded and creative. It allows your mind to relax – to think beyond the task at hand. When you detach yourself from the immediate situation, you're able to reflect internally. This reflection makes you more receptive to ideas generated within your subconscious, giving you the potential to create connections between ideas and concepts that you may not have otherwise recognized.

http://brolik.com/blog/daydreaming-key-creative-problem-solving/

Side Bar | Dreaming, Ideation & Problem Solving

The story of Elias Howe's invention of the sewing machine in 1845 is a case in point. Howe had been struggling to invent a machine that would sew with the same speed and efficiency as Hargreaves' and Cartwright's new machines would spin and weave, but with no success. As the tale goes, exhausted by frustration, Howe fell asleep at his workbench one night and had this dream:

He is in Africa, fleeing from cannibals through the jungle. Despite his frantic efforts to escape, the natives capture him, tie him up hand and foot, and carry him back to their village slung from a pole. There they dump him into a huge iron pot full of water. They light a fire under the pot and start to boil him alive.

As the water starts to bubble and boil around him, he discovers that the ropes have loosened enough for him to work his hands free. He tries repeatedly to take hold of the edge of the pot and haul himself out of the hot water, but every time he manages to heave himself up over the edge of the pot, the natives reach across over the flames and forcibly poke him back down into the pot again with their sharp spears.

When Howe awoke from this "nightmare," much of his mind was absorbed with sorting through the emotions of the dream-- but another part was able to note with objectivity, "That's odd-- those spears all have holes in the points...." As Howe came more fully awake, he thought, "Holes in the points... holes in the points! That's it! That's the answer!

As he awoke, Howe realized that the trick to making his sewing machine work was to move the thread transport hole up to point of the needle (as opposed to a handheld needle, where the hole is on the base). It then was a relatively simple matter to design a system of gears that would cause the needle to poke the thread down through the layers of cloth, wrap it around a second thread, and then pull it up again, all very neatly and efficiently. And with the invention of the sewing machine, the last bottleneck to the mechanical production of clothing was broken--this dream lead very directly to the realization of the industrial revolution!
http://www.jeremytaylor.com/dream_work/the_creative_impulse_in_dreams/

- **Einstein's Special Theory of Relativity**

Albert Einstein was always huge supporter of creativity, famously saying that "imagination is more important than knowledge." Perhaps he felt this way because he dreamed the Special Theory of Relativity when he was only a teenager. In the dream, he watched a farmer turn on an electric fence next to a herd of cows, and all of the cows appeared to jump backwards in shock at the same time. When he recounted what he had seen to the farmer, who had been standing on the opposite side of the field, the farmer explained that he had seen something different: The cows had jumped back one-by-one in order, not all at the same time. The message was clear: Events look different depending upon an individual's position, because of the time it takes light to reach the eyes. And poof! Inspiration for the Special Theory of Relativity was found.

http://themindunleashed.org/2014/09/dreaming-can-lead-amazing-creative-breakthroughs.html

Answer to the A / B picture set:
The distinction is the ovals are all pointing to the X in the A group, and the ovals area all pointing at the circles in the B group.

"If we all think alike, no one is thinking very much."
-*Walt Whitman*

Epilogue: Curtain Call

It's worth it to keep the embers glowing.

| 11 Reasons Why Every Company Should Have A Creative Thinking Workshop...At Least Once a Year

It was 2:45 a.m. when I laid my head to the pillow Thursday of last week. In the 15 plus years I've traveled through-out North America, it was one of the most challenging travel days in quite some time. After 3 flight cancellations and 3 delays, I finally arrived at Reagan National from Atlanta by way of Chicago only to be abandoned by the rental car service with yet another hour drive to my hotel.

With less that 5 hours of sleep, I would be on my way to a client site to conduct a full day workshop. Just from logic one would think that the end of this short travel saga would end in pure exhaustion as I returned to Atlanta 24 hours later. And yet, exactly the opposite occurred.

Luckily I was conducting one of my favorite workshops, "Creative & Innovative Thinking - The Next New Skill" (and this says a lot because I genuinely enjoy all of the topics I facilitate). And though I've done it often, this time it had a particular affect and meaning.

What I experienced in the next several hours really surprised me -- so much so it inspired this writing. Instead of feeling utterly exhausted, by the end of the day, I felt completely energized. And though I am aware of and market many of the obvious benefits of this topic (it's one of my most requested), I was re-reminded in a unique way of the multiple benefits of this learning experience. It compelled me to document and share the value of this topic even more!

Upon returning to my office, I wrote down how I was feeling and along with participant feedback documented the lingering results of the experience. I noted how I and others felt along with the activities that contributed to it...

- stimulated - using fun tools to draw, conceptualizing to activate imagination
- energized - interactive activities - releases endorphins and "feel good" hormones
- refreshed - good mental work-out
- inspired - results from some of the exercises that inspired more creativity in me, seeing what others came up with
- connected - activities in the creative process created a bonding experience
- challenged - revealed areas I could think differently, think better
- happy - had so much fun, laughed a lot
- satisfied - helping other people connect with their potential
- motivated - to produce
- empowered - feel more capable to contribute
- hopeful - there are more possibilities than I initially imagined

This list reflects the 11 reasons (and for sure there's more) why every company should have a creative thinking workshop at least once a year. Would you like for your staff to experience more of these qualities or even have them at all?

Of all the topics I've facilitated over the years, this one provides it's own unique experience and impact. It's memorable and tangible, both inspiring and practical and it's easy to demonstrate return-on-investment. Just ask yourself this question, "How much is an idea worth?" How much is teach your employees how to think worth?"

The Role & Power of Diversity in A Company's Competitive Edge

I mentioned many times the need and value for variety in what we know and how we experience the creative process. Those same principles and benefits also hold true in having a diverse workforce. The breath of diverse knowledge provides greater opportunity for better ideas.

That's why having a diverse workforce enhances a company's opportunity for growth and profitability.

When I think of team diversity I consider the content and segment from my team collaboration workshop entitled, *The Me in Team*. This section references the uniqueness of team members in terms of how they think, how they communicate as well as their beliefs and values, all of which were shaped during their formative years from a variety of sources.

Consider your values, beliefs, ways of thinking and communicating and how they were shaped through the influence of the items on the list to follow:
- Natural Wiring (personality)
- Family (ethnic, gender, birth order)
- Social
    - Hobbies
    - Neighborhood
    - Spiritual
    - Schools
    - Regional
    - Country of origin
    - Generation

- Work Life
  Jobs
  Industry
  Bosses
  Company

Of note, personality does play a key role (which also incorporates left or right brain orientation). Even if you have siblings, their experience with your parents were sometimes much different than yours. In fact in any situation, two people can have the exact same experience and interpret it in completely different ways. That's diversity at its core – perception and interpretation!

Diversity then becomes broader and more dimensional when the items on the list are more varied. It's wonderful to see this in action, which I get to experience in my workshops.

That variety offers the opportunity for great crosspollination to occur resulting in novel hybrids of products and services or unconventional solutions to some of your greatest challenges!

Here's a talent management, diversity revision of that popular insanity definition I referenced earlier:

"Hiring the same people over and over again and expecting different results."

Consider diversity part of your profit strategy. Remember, if everyone is singing the same note, there is no harmony or beauty in the music. As a singer I can unequivocally say, unison gets boring!

"I've never pained, never written, never taken photos, but I've always thought of myself as a creative person. Business is my canvas.
- Anita Roddick

"You cannot depend on your eyes when your imagination is out of focus."
- Mark Twain

About the Author

JoAnn R. Corley |
www.thehumansphere.com

JoAnn Corley is the Founder, CEO of The
Human Sphere™, a consultancy that helps
individuals and companies increase
earnings through holistic talent
management.

She is also a dynamic, inspiring speaker and author who has a
contagious passion for the topics she delivers. She has shared that
passion with thousands across North America on such themes as
creative thinking, team synergy, personal branding, emotional
intelligence and holistic talent management. She holds the unique
distinction of haven spoken in every major city and state in the U.S.

She is author of several books most recent of which is *15 Shifts – The
Essential Guide to Transform Your Talent Management* and the soon to
be released *Brain On Fire – Unleashing Your Creative Superpowers*. She
is also creator of the professional development app – The 1% Edge
Portable Coach, available on all smartphone platforms.

Additionally, she is contributing author to the book, Ordinary Women,
Extraordinary Success, a collaborative effort with some of the top female
motivational speakers in North American and hailed by Jack Canfield of
Chicken Soup for the Soul fame as a must read.

Named to the top 100 Most Social HR Experts on Twitter, Huffington
Post, you can find her on most social media platforms as well as radio
shows and online media across the country and internationally. She
has been quoted or featured in articles for NBC News, Monster.com,
Harvard Business Review, HR Hero, ASTD National, Management
Business Daily, to name a few, and has served as North America
Career Contributor for the Daily Telegraph UK.

Social Media Information:

Twitter   @joanncorley
Google+   https://plus.google.com/+JoAnnCorley
Facebook
https://www.facebook.com/joanncorley.the1percentcoach
LinkedIn   www.linkedin.com/in/joanncorley

Websites:
Speaker site-Blog: www.joanncorleyspeaks.com
Company site: www.thehumansphere.com
Professional
Development blog: www.the1percentedge.com

APP: The 1% Edge Portable Coach |
the1percentedgeapp.com (available on all
smart phone platforms)

| Books I've Read
Orbiting the Giant Hairball – Gordon MacKenize
Whack on the Side of the Head
Wake up Your Creative Genius
Brain Drain
Rise of the Creative Class – Richard Florida
The Creative Economy – John Howskins
Jump Start Your Business Ideas

| Other Resources
Luminosity

Other Books & Audios From JoAnn Corley
Check out JoAnn's Amazon Author's page:
http://www.amazon.com/JoAnn-R.-Corley/e/B004HGQKZ2

To book JoAnn for your next event:
Email: joann@thehumansphere.com

Toll Free: 888.388.0565

59999572R00061

Made in the USA
Charleston, SC
18 August 2016